SAMARITAN COOKBOOK

By Benyamim Tsedaka

Recipes from Batia bat Yefet Tsedaka & Zippora Sassoni Tsedaka

Edited by Ben Piven & Avishay Zelmanovich

Academic consultant: Steven Fine

Photographer: Yadid Levi

Creative designer: Sharon Yarimi Stein

Graphic designer: Neda Djavaherian

Inspired by the original work:

◆

נפלאות המטבח השומרוני

عجائب من المطبخ السامري

WONDERS OF
THE SAMARITAN KITCHEN

◆

ᵐᵇᵃᵠᵞᵃᵞᵚᵃ ᵃᵠᵍᵞᵃ

SAMARITAN
COOKBOOK

A CULINARY ODYSSEY
FROM THE ANCIENT ISRAELITES
TO THE MODERN MEDITERRANEAN

CONTENTS

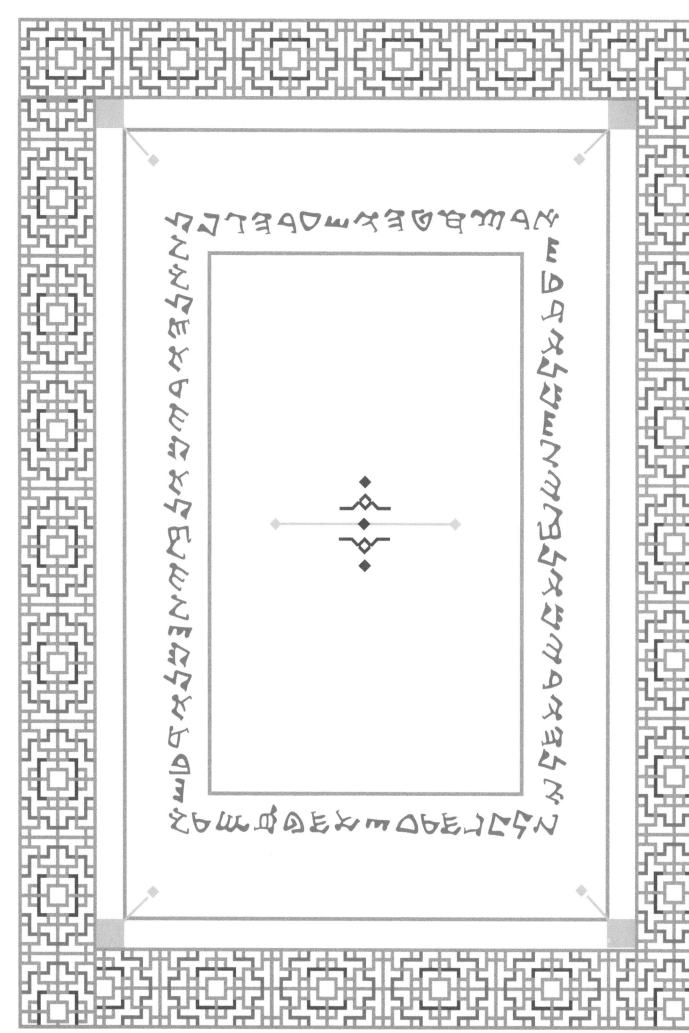

The Samaritan Cookbook reaches into the kitchens and dining rooms of the Samaritan people, descendants of the northern Kingdom of Israel. They have enjoyed 3,000 continuous years of tasty Holy Land cuisine.

INTRODUCTION

BY BEN PIVEN

The Samaritan Cookbook is a culinary odyssey from the ancient Middle East to the modern Levant. We are building an edible cultural bridge uniting diverse traditions. Featuring Samaritan history as a unique phenomenon at the intersection of the Israeli and Palestinian experiences, as well as the Hebrew and Arabic spheres, we celebrate the common foods eaten by many peoples.

This book will appeal to five main groups: Mediterranean food lovers who want good, healthy cuisine; coexistence supporters interested in bringing Middle Eastern communities together; Jewish people fascinated by a distinct Israelite heritage; Christians hoping to connect with a biblical legacy; and scholars studying this one-of-a-kind ethnolinguistic sect.

The delicious dishes described here are grouped into starters, mains, desserts, and more. Each recipe includes directions, commentary, and beautiful photography that offers us access to the world of the Samaritans. We explain broader cultural references and honor the legacy of the Samaritan cooks who originally put the instructions on paper. We also present the beauty of holiday celebrations – Sukkot and Passover, important festivals from the Five Books of Moses – and give contextual descriptions about their special meaning. The style of the Samaritan Cookbook fuses old and new, giving a modern feel to 3,000-year-old motifs.

The team behind the Samaritan Cookbook is New York-based. Avishay Zelmanovich and I envisioned this effort as a contemporary version adapted from the original 2011 cookbook put together by Holon, Israel-based Benyamim Tsedaka, a Samaritan jack-of-all-trades who serves as their chief academician. The community itself is split between that southern suburb of Tel Aviv, and the town of Kiryat Luza, just outside the Palestinian city of Nablus on the slopes of Mt. Gerizim in the West Bank.

Enter a world where parchment and lamb sacrifice take on new meaning in the 21st century. We aspire to help teach new cooking techniques, explore uncharted gastronomic terrain, and give curious fans an appreciation of largely unknown Samaritan culinary richness and depth.

PROLOGUE

BY BENYAMIM TSEDAKA

There are many different expressions of a people's culture: their history, poetry, literature, tradition and heritage. In addition to all of those, there is one that we must include, and that is a people's food culture. The uniqueness of a people within the world community can be measured by the way they bequeath their special tastes onto the wider world.

We Israelite Samaritans have a unique experience through a long, tumultuous past spanning thousands of years. We still carry out the same annual festivals, as well as visits to holy places during days of happiness and days of mourning. Our days of flourishing and good fortune, as well as days of withering, all in the Land of Israel, give us continued hope that we will last forever.

One of the most important parts of Samaritan identity is our special cuisine delivered by our ancient forefathers - from the days when the menu and ingredients were quite sparse, to the days that it became enriched with hundreds of different kinds of spices and dishes. From this extensive kitchen, we have selected a few dozen of the best dishes, all of them an expression of over 3,000 years of Israelite history. These dishes are influenced by this narrow strip of land in the Levant that connects the cultures of Africa, Asia, and Europe - with a special Samaritan touch.

The wonders and aromas of the Samaritan kitchen arise from the pages of this cookbook. Some of the dishes are Israelite, others are uniquely Samaritan, and a portion are imported dishes from other food cultures. The tastes crystallized to make all those who eat them lick their fingers at the end of each meal.

There are readers who will note that some of the dishes that grace these pages can also be tasted in the Palestinian kitchen. That culinary tradition developed from the same roots as the ancient Israelite kitchen. The commonalities that exist between the two can be expressed in two words: very tasty!

"IF YOU ARE ASKED WHETHER YOU KNOW HOW TO
PREPARE A CERTAIN DISH, ALWAYS ANSWER THAT YOU
CAN. EVEN IF YOU DON'T KNOW HOW, YOU WILL LEARN
ALONG THE WAY."

Samaritan Proverb

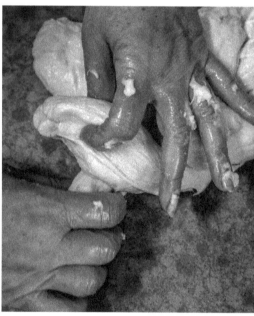

Our food relies heavily on fresh ingredients. Fresh foods and vegetables from the fields and the garden: chicken, turkey, sheep, cattle, kosher fish, baked goods, dairy and cheese dishes, and preserved vegetables. All of these come fresh from the market, never frozen, but directly from the hands of the butcher and farmer to the kitchen, and from there to the table.

The manuscript of the original Hebrew version of this book was written by two sisters; my late mother Batia bat Yefet Tsedaka and Zippora Sassoni Tsedaka, both career educators who also raised glorious families. We have edited and arranged the recipes in order to more easily impart upon the world these special Samaritan dishes.

Batia Tsedaka left our world on on April 20, 2010. The original Hebrew version was presented to the members of the Samaritan community on the first anniversary of her passing during Passover 2011. The goal then – and now – is for the book to be used in every Samaritan household and far beyond. Thanks to Professor Steven Fine and the Yeshiva University Israelite Samaritans Project for helping us to realize that dream.

The Samaritan Cookbook is dedicated to enshrining the progressive status of all Samaritan women, including the 23 Samaritan women who contributed their best tasting recipes and enthuse the palate with their wonderful dishes. I would like to express my deep gratitude and respect as the primary author.

Come to the table • صحتين • Bon appetit • בתיאבון

ᨅᨖᨆᨑᨖ ᨑᨎᨖᨆᨖᨎ ᨑᨔᨅᨋᨌ ᨐᨑᨆᨌᨑ ᨌᨉ ᨖᨆᨐ
ᨅᨖᨆᨑᨖ ᨑᨎᨖᨆᨖᨎ ᨑᨑᨆᨑᨎ ᨆᨋ ᨑᨍᨖᨆᨑᨎ ᨌᨉ ᨖᨆᨐ

THE SAMARITAN PANTRY

ANISE

Similar to fennel and licorice, it is commonly found in Southwest Asia. From food and drink to candies, the sweet flavor is characteristic of the region. In tea, anise helps with digestion. Anise is used to make arak, a liquor similar to raki, ouzo, sambuca, pastis, and aguardiente.

ARABIC SPICES

Commonly known as Baharat, this spice blend often consists of allspice, black pepper, cardamom, cinnamon, cloves, coriander, cumin, ginger, nutmeg, and paprika. From Turkey to the Gulf, it can be used as a condiment or to season chicken, beef, lamb, and fish.

CORIANDER

Found across the Mediterranean basin and also known as cilantro, the dried seeds and fresh leaves of the plant are widely used in many cuisines. Heating up the seeds makes them more aromatic and pungent for cooking.

CUMIN

The ground seeds of this flowering plant native to the eastern Mediterranean are used in the cuisines of many cultures. Said to make its way into the food of the Semitic world from the Sumerians, the seeds can be grown in dry, subtropical environments. With its unique taste, the flavor gives off a sense of earthiness and warmth. Cumin is larger and lighter than caraway, with which it is often confused. With many health benefits, cumin helps digestion, improves immunity, and can be used to treat a variety of other common maladies.

PAPRIKA

Originally from the New World — not from Hungary — the deep-red spice is made from the air-dried fruits of chili pepper. In Samaritan cuisine, it is often used as garnish for hummus, labneh, and yoghurt dishes. Paprika is also a key part of shakshuka for breakfast and many maftoul grain recipes.

TURMERIC

Popular in India and the Middle East, the mustard-colored spice is somewhat bitter and hot. Also considered to have healing powers, it is used in Levantine semolina cakes. Turmeric comes either fresh or in powder form, which is three times more potent. The flavor is commonly included in soups and rice dishes.

ZA'ATAR

Unique to the Levant, za'atar refers to a spice mixture whose prized main ingredient is alternatively called Biblical hyssop and Lebanese/Syrian oregano. Also related to thyme and basil, the herb blend generally includes sesame seeds, sumac, salt, and marjoram. Za'atar is often served with pita and olive oil, in addition to baked goods, salads, meats, and in tea. You can find za'atar at your favorite spice seller, or even make your own at home after mastering the right proportions!

SAMARITAN ALPHABET

The Samaritan alphabet is used for sacred purposes – mostly to write religious text in Samaritan Hebrew, including the Torah. In this book about food, we feature six especially meaningful and relevant Bible verses written in this script.

These ancient letters are a variant of what modern scholars call the Old or Paleo-Hebrew alphabet, derived from proto-Canaanite and similar to Phoenician, that the Judeans also used prior to taking on the Imperial Aramaic script during the sixth century BCE.

Samaritans in Nablus speak Palestinian Arabic, and the community in Holon speaks modern Hebrew. Arabic has 28 letters, six more than are shown with the letter equivalents at right – since the Hebrew alphabets have just 22 letters.

Four letters in the Samaritan alphabet diverged from the earlier Semitic sounds: baa (vav / waw); iy (he / heh); it (Het / Hah); and in (ayin / ain).

Clock-wise from top: Gezer Calendar, 10th century BCE;
half-shekel coin 67 CE; Samaritan mezuzah; Holon street sign

LETTER CHART

Semitic Sounds	Samaritan Letter Names	Samaritan Hebrew	Old Hebrew	Jewish Hebrew	Arabic Equivalent
A	alaf	𐤀	𐤀	א	ا
B	bit	𐤁	𐤁	ב	ب
G	gaman	𐤂	𐤂	ג	جَ
D	dalat	𐤃	𐤃	ד	د
H	iy	𐤄	𐤄	ה	ه
W	baa	𐤅	𐤅	ו	و
Z	zen	𐤆	𐤆	ז	ز
Hh	it	𐤇	𐤇	ח	خ
Th	tit	𐤈	𐤈	ט	ط
Y	yut	𐤉	𐤉	י	ي
K	kaaf	𐤊	𐤊	כ	ك
L	labat	𐤋	𐤋	ל	ل
M	mim	𐤌	𐤌	מ	م
N	nun	𐤍	𐤍	נ	ن
S	singaat	𐤎	𐤎	ס	س
Ay	in	𐤏	𐤏	ע	ع
F	fi	𐤐	𐤐	פ	ف
Ts	tsaadiy	𐤑	𐤑	צ	ص
Q	quf	𐤒	𐤒	ק	ق
R	rish	𐤓	𐤓	ר	ر
Sh	shan	𐤔	𐤔	ש	ش
T	taaf	𐤕	𐤕	ת	ت

אֶרֶץ חִטָּה וּשְׂעֹרָה גֶּפֶן וּתְאֵנָה וְרִמּוֹן אֶרֶץ זֵית שֶׁמֶן וּדְבָשׁ

A LAND OF WHEAT, AND BARLEY, AND GRAPEVINES,
AND FIG TREES, AND POMEGRANATES; A LAND OF OLIVE
OIL AND HONEY.

DEUTERONOMY 8:8
(SAMARITAN VERSION)

SUKKOT

The biblical holiday of Sukkot, "booths" or "tabernacles" in Hebrew, is festive and colorful. In the Samaritan tradition, a sukkah is constructed inside the home and symbolizes dwelling in the wilderness and cherishing the fruits of the heavens. It is even reminiscent of the Garden of Eden.

Samaritans use four types of plants — "beautiful fruit", palm fronds, leafy branches, and willows of the brook — to build the sukkah.

The fruits are suspended from the sukkah frame and can weigh up to 800 pounds. They are arranged impeccably in amazing geometric designs — elliptical, circular, and square.

Most Samaritans use the same metal frame every year, in addition to wire mesh, plastic brackets, and four strong poles. Usually, the girls of the house attach brass wires to each piece of fruit, before the children line up and pass the fruits to teenagers and young adults who hang the fall produce — all the while singing a Samaritan sukkah-building song.

The elaborate patterns are put together according to a plan that has been decided in advance. From grapefruits, lemons, and quinces to apples, peaches, and peppers, the decorative elements are sometimes complemented by colored paper and electric lights.

Samaritan high priests decided many centuries ago to move the sukkot indoors, as the structures were calling attention to the community during times of persecution.

Nowadays built in Samaritan living rooms, people do not sit directly underneath the fruit due to the dangers of falling pomelos and eggplants!

The Samaritans — in keeping with the ancient Israelite calendar (Exodus 12) — begin the new year each spring, just before Passover. So, the Sukkot autumn harvest festival is the third of three pilgrimages to Mt. Gerizim, following Passover and Shavuot — Pentecost — seven weeks later.

After the morning pilgrimage to the summit of Mt. Gerizim on the first day of Sukkot, Samaritans descend from the sacred mountain to eat a meal near the family sukkah. On the first and final (eighth) day of the festival (as on the Sabbath), Samaritans serve their food cold – to assert the holiness of the sacred day, when it is forbidden to do labor or light a fire.

Samaritans enjoy the holiday by drinking arak, an alcoholic beverage made of aniseed. When mixed with water, the clear alcohol turns milky white. They also consume khshaff, a delicacy made from apricot, almond, and pomegranate juice.

While listening to Sukkot melodies, the Samaritans eat a wide variety of salads, almonds, and beans. To add sweetness to the occasion, baked goods include ma'amul, a sesame anise cake, and baklava.

On the eighth day of Sukkot, known as *Shemini Atzeret*, Samaritan communal worship begins after midnight and lasts for nine hours. According to the community's lore, that is when the gates of heaven open up and angels come down to gather prayers.

The priests, *Kohanim* in Hebrew, raise up the Torah scrolls and allow each worshiper to touch the metal cases. After this ritual comes the blessing of the whole congregation, as the priest waves the Torah and Samaritans cover their faces with their right palms. This gesture is a reminder of Moses's hand motion when he looked upon God in the burning bush.

ולקחתם לכם ביום הראשון פרי עץ הדר כפות תמרים
וענפי עץ עבת וערבי נחל ושמחתם
לפני ה' אלהיכם שבעת ימים

ON THE FIRST DAY, YOU SHALL TAKE THE FRUIT OF
A BEAUTIFUL TREE, PALM FRONDS, BRANCHES OF
A LEAFY TREE, AND WILLOWS OF THE BROOK. YOU
SHALL REJOICE BEFORE THE LORD YOUR GOD FOR
SEVEN DAYS.

LEVITICUS 23:40
(SAMARITAN VERSION)

Samaritans eat the holy fruits of the sukkah after the festival. They squeeze the fruit into sweet juice and love to make marmalade from giant citrons, known as *etrogim*.

After the holiday, the Samaritans gather up the dry leaves of each sukkah and burn them in bonfires, to commemorate the retaking of Mt. Gerizim from the Byzantine empire nearly fifteen hundred years ago. The mountain was lost to the Samaritans at several points in Samaritan history.

This symbolic ritual keeps alive the story of how the legendary leader Baba Rabbah ("great father" in Aramaic) and his nephew Levi fought to take the most sacred Samaritan place on the festival of Sukkot.

Samaritans have an open-sukkah policy and this festival is a great time to visit the community.

STARTERS

Avocado & Sesame Dip

سلطة افوكادو بطحينة   סלט אבוקדו עם טחינה

INGREDIENTS

1 big avocado

2 tbsp tahini

2 crushed garlic cloves

3 tbsp lemon juice

3 tbsp water

½ tbsp salt

1 small tomato

12 pitted black olives

This appetizer is like guacamole with a Middle Eastern twist, and goes well while you're waiting for the rest of the food. Thoroughly mash the avocado with a fork, then add all the other ingredients except the olives and tomato. Move the dip onto a plate and garnish with the olives and tomato. If you want to add more decoration, use some chopped coriander or mint leaves, along with pitted black olives.

"BEHIND EVERY SUCCESSFUL MAN STANDS A WOMAN!"

Samaritan Proverb

Samaritan Hummus

حمص   חומוס

◆ ——————— ◆

INGREDIENTS

4 cups cooked chickpeas

Half-filled cup boiling water

3 heaping tbsp tahini

2 crushed cloves garlic

Juice from one whole lemon

⅓ tsp of salt

¼ tsp cumin

¼ tsp quarter paprika

Tomato cut into half circles

Pickle cut into slices

20 black olives

¼ cup olive oil

Throw all of the ingredients together into a food processor. Blend for a total of five minutes. Lift the top, and if it's too clumpy, then continue blending for two minutes. Spread the blend onto a plate and garnish with cumin and paprika.

Take any leftover cooked chickpeas, with water strained out, and add on top. Decorate the plate with tomato and pickle slices on the edge of the plate, in addition to black olives.

Zucchini with Yogurt

سلطة كوسة بلبن   סלט קישואים עם יוגורט

INGREDIENTS

1 big zucchini or 2 small
zucchinis

1 clove garlic

1 tsp salt

1 ½ small yogurt containers
(about 10 oz.)

Pinch of paprika

Cumin

Chopped parsley

Frying oil

Black olives

Roast the zucchini in the oven in a baking bag with the cooking oil. Let the zucchini cool down, peel it, and squeeze out the juices. Mash up the insides in a bowl and add crushed garlic, salt, and the yogurt. Mix up the ingredients and stir them up before adding the spices. Use the parsley, cumin, and paprika according to your personal taste, and then put the black olives on the side for decoration. It should be ready to enjoy for the whole family.

Egg and Okra Quiche

بمية مقلية مع بيض   פשטידת במיה וביצים

INGREDIENTS

3 lbs of okra

4 eggs

salt

¼ tsp Arabic spices

oil for frying

Wash the okra, cut them into 2-3 pods each, and fry them in a pan on the stove. Crack the eggs into a bowl and whisk them. Add 1 teaspoon of salt and a quarter teaspoon of Arabic spices. Take the fried okra and put the pieces evenly spread out into a Pyrex pan. Pour the eggs into the pan over the okra. Place into the oven at 350 Fahrenheit for 20 minutes. Then place the finished product onto the table, but watch out, it will be hot!

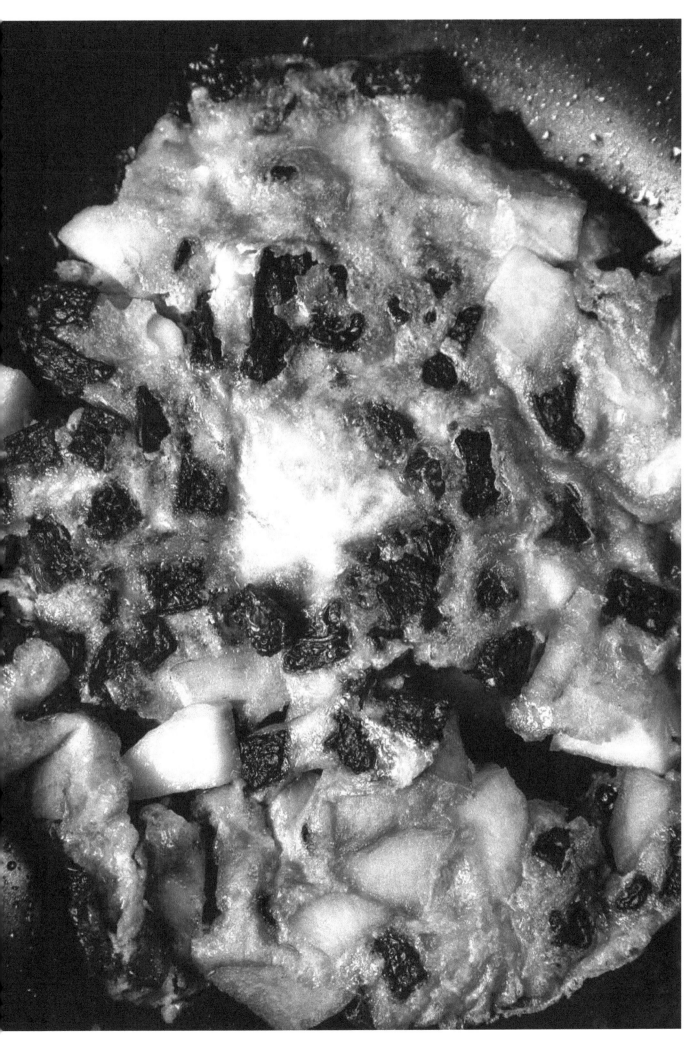

Eggplant with Pomegranate Juice

بابا غنوج بعصير الرمان   חצילים במיץ רימונים

INGREDIENTS

1 big eggplant or 2 small
eggplants
1 crushed clove garlic
¼ tsp salt
1 tbsp lemon juice
¼ cup pomegranate juice
A few strands of parsley
A couple black olives
Olive oil
A few chopped mint leaves

Roast the eggplants, and then take the skin off and mash up the insides in a bowl. Add salt, garlic, lemon juice, and pomegranate juice. Taste test and fiddle with the balance of ingredients. Put on either a flat plate or a regular plate and decorate. Sprinkle with olive oil and you're good to go.

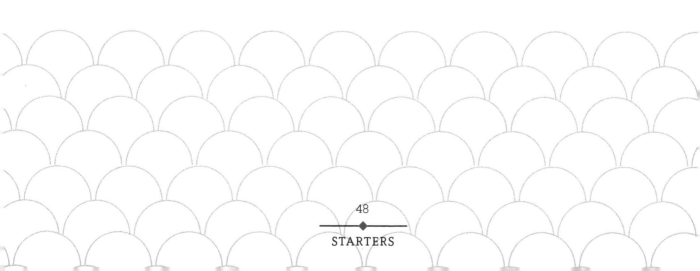

Spiced Thistle

سلطة عكوب متبلة   סלט עכובית מתובל

INGREDIENTS

2 cups of thistle*

2 tbsp lemon juice

2 cloves crushed garlic

1 tsp salt

¼ cup chopped coriander

½ tsp sumac

1 tbsp olive oil

To prepare, cut off the spikes with scissors. Wash and cut the thistle into small pieces. Cook in water until it gets soft. Strain the thistle and put into a bowl with the rest of the ingredients. Mix up everything before adding the olive oil and mixing a bit more. Then place onto a plate before presenting.

*Outside the Levant, tumble thistle (gundelia) is hard to find. But other similar plants can be used in its place.

Red Cabbage Salad

سلطة ملفوف أحمر   סלט כרוב אדום

INGREDIENTS

1 lb red cabbage

½ lb radish

3-4 scallions

½ tsp salt

2 tbsps lemon juice

2 tsp corn oil

½ cup thinly chopped parsley

Rinse the vegetables well, and then cut the cabbage into thin slices. Crush the radish, and throw on a pinch of salt. Add in chopped scallions, lemon juice, parsley, and corn oil. Mix it thoroughly, and present on a flat plate to be served to your guests. Additionally, you can add a few olives.

MAINS

Bulgur Wheat

برغل مقلي   בורגול במתכונת אורז, רצוי קלוי

◆ ——————— ◆

INGREDIENTS

2 cups of bulgur wheat

1 chopped onion

1 tsp safflower oil

1 cup of chickpeas soaked
overnight in water

1 tsp salt

½ tsp Arabic spices

⅓ cup corn oil

5 cups water

After you've culled the bulgur, wash it off, and strain it. Put all of the oil in a cooking pan and fry up the chopped onions until they become golden. Add the bulgur and continue frying for another 10 minutes. Add five cups of water, along with the safflower oil, chickpeas, salt, and Arabic spices into the pan. When the water reaches a boil, lower the heat and continue cooking until all the water is absorbed. Then just add the bulgur wheat to a plate and present it to your eager guests. Often the dish also includes chopped almonds.

Cauliflower with Rice - Maqlouba

مقلوبة قرنبيط   כרובית עם אורז - מקלובה

INGREDIENTS

1 head of cauliflower, halved

2 cups of rice

4 ½ cups water

1 tbsp cumin

1 tsp safflower

1 big onion

5 cloves of garlic

Oil

2 tbsp salt

Some versions of maqlouba are with meat, but this one is vegetarian. Take the leaves and stems off the cauliflower, and then place them in a pot with salt. Fill with water until the items are covered completely. Keep on medium heat until it boils. Turn off the flame and let sit for a few minutes and then strain the cauliflower. Take out the big and medium-sized flowers and put them on a frying pan with oil until they become yellow. Afterwards take them out of the pan and place them into a fireproof pot. Add a teaspoon of oil, the onion chopped thoroughly, and the garlic sliced along its length, as well as the cumin, safflower, and salt.

Place the pan on medium flame until it boils. Wash the rice and add it to the boiling pot. You can enhance the taste if any additional spices are needed. Gently stir and cover again. Lower the heat to a minimum and let it boil. Repeat stirring and cover. Wait until the rice becomes soft and all the flavors are absorbed. Now you've got a super tasty casserole meal for everyone to enjoy.

Tomatoes with Beef – Kalieh

قلايه   עגבניות עם קוביות בשר

INGREDIENTS

2 lbs red tomatoes

1 tbsp tomato puree

1 cup of beef cubes

2 cups of almonds

1 tbsp pine nuts

2 tbsp oil

Arabic spices

1 onion

2-3 cloves garlic

Salt

Cut an x into the bottom of the tomatoes and then drop the tomatoes into a pot of boiling water for 1-2 minutes. Remove them from the water, then peel, and chop the tomatoes into small cubes. Halve, peel, and lightly pan fry the almonds. Pan fry the pine nuts separately. Thoroughly cut the onions, and then pan fry with garlic after slicing along the length of the cloves. Then add the cubed tomatoes into the pan. Add a teaspoon of salt to the mix. Then they'll become soft and the fluids will come out. Add the beef cubes and continue cooking until the juices mostly evaporate. Add the almond and pine nuts into the same pan, continue cooking for another 5 minutes. Now add the tomato puree and Arabic spices, and continue for another five minutes. Put onto a serving plate and you're done!

"AN ORDERLY AND FINE WOMAN, FINE DISHES, AND TASTY
FOOD PLEASE THE DINERS AT THE TABLE"

Samaritan Proverb

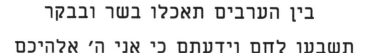

בין הערבים תאכלו בשר ובבקר

תשבעו לחם וידעתם כי אני ה׳ אלהיכם

BY EVENING YOU SHALL EAT MEAT, AND IN THE MORNING
YOU SHALL HAVE YOUR FILL OF BREAD, AND YOU WILL
KNOW THAT I AM THE LORD YOUR GOD.

EXODUS 16:12

(SAMARITAN VERSION)

Potatoes Stuffed with Lamb

محشي بططا مع فرم   תפוחי אדמה ממולאים בבשר

INGREDIENTS

10 medium-sized potatoes

1 cup of cubed lamb meat

1 tbsp pine nuts

1 onion

Salt

Black pepper

Cinnamon

2 tbsp tomato paste

Oil

Peel the potatoes, and wash them well. Slice the top off of each potato so it can be used later as a lid. Then scoop out the potatoes to create pockets in the middle so they can hold what comes next. Lightly pan fry the lamb cubes, the onion, and the pine nuts together. Then put everything in a bowl and add the rest of the spices. Then put the filling into the potatoes. Put the potato lids on, and use toothpicks to hold them together. Lightly pan fry or put into the oven the potatoes before placing them all in a Pyrex tray.

Mix the tomato paste with 1½ cups of water, then pour this over all the potatoes in the pan. Cover the pan with aluminum foil, cook in the oven at 400 degrees Fahrenheit. Once everything smells just right and has begun looking slightly burnt, then take it out, and serve it up.

Chicken with Za'atar

دجاج مع الزعتر   עוף בזעתר

INGREDIENTS

1 whole chicken

3 tbsp zaatar

¼ cup olive oil

½ tbsp salt

½ tbsp English pepper

Slice open the chicken breast or alternatively cut between the thigh and the breast. Keep the back intact. Place the chicken upside down in a strainer. Pour salt and pepper on the chicken and leave it for 15 minutes. Mix the za'atar with the olive oil and glaze the chicken with that zaatar-oil blend.

With whatever is left of that blend, pour it into the middle of the chicken. Put one tablespoon of oil onto a baking pan, and then place the chicken into the pan. Preheat the oven to 400 degrees Fahrenheit and insert the pan into the oven for a half-hour after covering it with aluminum foil. For the last five minutes of cooking, peel up the aluminum foil so that the chicken browns a bit. Then your chicken should be ready for prime time, best served alongside potatoes, carrots, or other vegetables.

Lamb Meatballs with Pine Nuts

فرم مع صنوبر   קוביות בשר כבש בצנוברים

INGREDIENTS

1-2 cups of cubed lamb meat

2 tbsp pine nuts

Allspice

Cinnamon

Salt

2 tbsp olive oil

Put the 2 tablespoons of oil in a pan and then lightly fry the pine nuts. When finished, put the pine nuts on a plate. Add the cubes into the pan and lightly pan fry them before adding 2/3 cups of water. Lower the stove flame to a minimum so the meat softens and the juices evaporate. Add the pine nuts and all the spices into the pan towards the end once the liquid is mostly gone. Mix well and let cook for another few moments. Feel free to garnish with little bits of parsley. Then the dish should be ready to present.

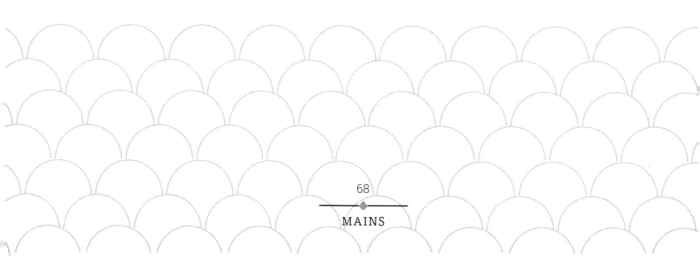

"KNOW THAT LOVE IS TRANSMITTED THROUGH THE STOMACH"

Samaritan Proverb

Couscous - Maftoul

مفتول   קוסקוס - מפתול

♦ ——————— ♦

INGREDIENTS

½ cup bulgur

3 lbs wheat flour

Boiled water with salt

1 cup of oil

Put the bulgur in a big bowl. With your right hand, mix the bulgur and add flour to the bulgur. Do it slowly, and it's best to mix water into the flour here and there. The morsels of bulgur should coagulate and gain in size until they become about the same diameter as chickpeas. Afterward, add oil quickly and make sure each granule is covered so that they don't stick together. Put the granules on a net above boiling water and steam them. Once poured out onto a tray, the large-grain couscous can be served with a variety of sauces, spices, meats, and vegetables.

Haifa Majadara

مجدرة حيفاوية   מג'דרה חיפאית

INGREDIENTS

1 ¼ cup brown lentils

½ cup rice

3 big onions

½ tsp safflower

1 tsp salt

5 cups water

Soak the rice overnight. Chop and lightly pan fry the onions. Cook the lentils in the 5 cups of water until they become soft. Add the rice and half the pan-fried onions, as well as the safflower and salt. Continue until it thickens and is ready to eat.

Samaritan Falafel

فلافل سامري   פלאפל שומרוני

♦ ——— ♦

INGREDIENTS

1 pound chickpeas

½ bag chopped parsley

½ bag coriander

1 clove garlic

1 onion

1-2 tbsp wheat flour

1 tsp cumin

1 tsp Arabic spices

1 tsp cinnamon

1 tsp salt

oil for frying

Soak the chickpeas in water for 12 hours. Drain and wash them well. Put them in a pot on the stove until the water begins to boil. Then drain out the water and mash up the chickpeas in a blender with garlic and onion. Add the coriander and parsley with the flour, all spices, and seasoning. Make balls out of the mix and then deep fry them in oil.

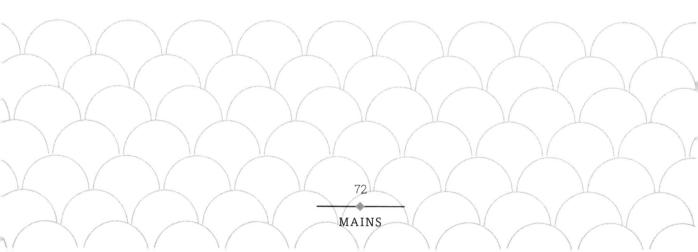

Stuffed Cabbage

ملفوف محشي   כרוב ממולא

INGREDIENTS

1 medium head cabbage

1 ½ cups of rice

2 cups of cubed meat

2 tbsp of pan-fried pine nuts

3-4 tbsp of tomato puree

½ tsp safflower

1 tsp salt

1 tbsp cumin

3 tbsp oil

Seasoning

Mint

Garlic

Boil some water in a medium pot. Separate out the cabbage leaves from the cabbage. Place them in hot water and then quickly rinse off with cold water. Lay the cabbage leaves flat. Divide each leaf into pieces. If the leaf isn't big, into two pieces. If the leaf is big, into three pieces. The area of each bit of filling should be three inches by three inches regardless of the exact shape. Lightly pan fry the meat cubes. Put a tablespoon of filling on every cabbage strip. Roll and close the sides of each cabbage leaf. Arrange them in a pot in layers. Place over high heat and then add 2 tablespoons of oil. Add half a teaspoon of salt and 1 tablespoon of cumin. Add water until the leaves are covered. Boil on medium heat. After they reach boiling temperature, lower the heat until all the water evaporates. Increase the heat until the leaves on the bottom burn slightly.

Preparing the sauce: Mix 3-4 heaping tablespoons of tomato puree with 1-2 cups of water. Add 1 teaspoon of mint and 1 clove of crushed garlic. Boil until the sauce begins to thicken. Pour one quarter of the sauce onto the leaves and continue to cook for another five minutes. Afterward, move all the contents of the pot into a tray, and then pour the rest of the sauce onto the cabbage in the tray.

Eggplant Stuffed with Sesame Paste

باذنجان محشي بطحينة   חצילים ממולאים ברוטב טחינה

◆ ——————— ◆

INGREDIENTS

2 lbs of small eggplant
(around 12 smallish ones)

1 cup of rice

1 tsp of safflower/saffron

¼ spoons of seasoning

1 tsp salt

5 tbsp oil

For sauce:

1 cup tahini

½ cup water

½ cup chopped coriander

2 cloves garlic

¼ tsp salt

Wash the eggplants. Don't peel them, but do take out the insides.

Preparing the filling: In a bowl, put all the rice. Then, wash and drain, and let sit for 15 minutes. Wash it again, then add safflower, black pepper and salt. Mix well. Add two tablespoons of oil and mix again. Hold the eggplant in your hand, and fill each until a third of the space is filled. Arrange them in a non-stick pot. Add to the pot 2-3 tablespoons of oil and arrange one layer of eggplant. Add around 1 ½ cups of water. Cook at the beginning on high heat and continue on medium heat until all the eggplant absorbs the water and you start to hear them crackle.

Preparing the sauce: Mix one cup of tahini with water. Add chopped coriander, crushed garlic, and salt, then mix them well. After they finish cooking, move the eggplants to an oven-proof pan. Pour the sauce over the eggplants, then place them into the preheated 400 degrees F oven for 15 minutes.

Vegetable Medley

خضروات مشكلة   מעורבת מחלוטה

INGREDIENTS

½ lbs fava beans

1 eggplant cut into small cubes

2 potatoes cut into small cubes

1 head of cauliflower broken up

1 big onion finely chopped

4 oz. tomato paste

1 ½ cups water

Salt

Black pepper

Oil

Lightly pan fry all four vegetables separately until they golden. Place them into a teflon pot and sprinkle in a half teaspoon of salt. Mix in the tomato paste and the water. Allow the water to come to a slow boil and then lower the heat and let simmer for another 15 minutes. Pour out most of the excess liquid and then put back onto the stove until all of the liquid has evaporated. Once that happens and the vegetables begin to sizzle, then it should be ready to serve. Feel free to add in the pepper at the end.

Beef Noodle Casserole

كباب ومعكرونة   פשטידת מקרונים וכבב בשר

INGREDIENTS

1 lbs ground beef

1 lbs straight macaroni

salt

allspice

1 tsp cinnamon

1 small onion

1 clove garlic

½ bag parsley

2 tbsp tomato paste

After bringing water to a boil and adding salt, pour in the noodles. Cook for five minutes, strain the water, and cool off with tap water. Put half the noodles into a pyrex pan, and flatten them evenly across the bottom. In a bowl, mix together the ground beef with all the spices, including salt, allspice, cinnamon, onion, garlic and parsley. Then cook on a stove until the meat is decently done. Add the kebab over that first layer, then add the second layer of macaroni. Mix the tomato paste with two cups of water and pour it on top of the macaroni. Cover the pan with aluminum foil. Preheat the oven to 400 degrees Fahrenheit. Insert the pan into the oven for 20 minutes.

FOOD CUSTOMS

The Samaritans observe complex dietary customs.

Scripture teaches the Israelite Samaritans not to eat any combination of milk and meat. This is based on Exodus 23:19, which prohibits the cooking of a young goat in the milk of its mother.

Samaritans wait six hours between eating milk and meat, and three hours between eating meat and milk.

Only Israelite Samaritan butchers may prepare ritually acceptable meat.

The Samaritan high priests and Sages say that 17 kinds of meat may be eaten, including chicken, turkey, quail, and dove. Goose and duck are forbidden because they have webbed feet. Pork, of course, is not to be eaten.

Of animals that walk on four legs, Samaritans eat sheep, goat, deer, and beef.

In keeping with Leviticus 11:3, animals to be eaten must have split hooves and chew their cud. Some species of locust and grasshopper are also permissible, as are fish with fins and scales.

Top: in Kiryat Luza, author Benyamim Tsedaka enjoys a tasty meal cooked by Mayas, Hadiya, and Furyal Cohen, who are pictured, left to right, at bottom.

DESSERTS

Kunafeh

كنافة   כנאפה מתוקה

◆ ——————— ◆

INGREDIENTS

2 lbs of shredded filo dough
known as "kataifi"

1 cup of oil

1 lbs of either almonds, hazelnuts, or pistachios (all peeled)

½ lbs pine nuts

1 ½ lbs sugar

Lemon juice from ½ lemon

For festive occasions or holidays, this is a great dessert. The tradition is that it's served on the third Sabbath of the 11th month (Shevat) to commemorate the Biblical story of Moses and Aaron reuniting after a long time. It also symbolizes the transition in the Samaritan calendar from winter to spring and the blossoming of flowers as nature becomes greener after the cold months. Sweets such as kunafeh and baklava are handed out after finishing the Sabbath morning service.

Pour the cup of oil on a baking pan. Add 1 lbs of dough and break it up into small pieces. Grind up all the nuts, then take one fifth of the ground nuts, as well as all of the pine nuts, and put them in a separate pan. The remainder of the ground nuts should be sprinkled over the dough. You should make sure to leave room on the edges of the dough. Now add and break up the remaining 1 lbs of dough on top. Insert the baking pan into an oven that has been preheated to 355 Fahrenheit for twenty minutes or until the bottom of the kunafeh turns brown. While the kunafeh is in the oven, pan fry the nuts we set aside in a separate pan.

Bring out a bigger baking pan, take the kunafeh out of the oven and turn it over onto the bigger baking pan so that the browned bottom is now on the top. Sprinkle the pan-fried nuts on top. Cook all of the sugar and 1 ½ cups of water, combined with the juice from ½ a lemon and cook it until the mix thickens. When it comes together, pour it onto the kunafeh in an even fashion. Some Samaritans like their kunafeh with cheese, preferably homemade from goat's or sheep's milk. You can place this layer of soft white cheese on top of the dough, once it's in the baking pan. Let it melt sufficiently before putting the other ingredients above the cheese.

Ma'amul

معمول   מעמול

INGREDIENTS

2 lbs flour

1 lbs semolina

3 cups of oil

1 ½ cups water

½ tsp gum arabic

3 tsp of baking powder

Pinch of salt

For the stuffing:

1 box of pitted dates

Mash up the dates.

½ lbs hazelnuts or almonds

¼ tsp cinnamon

2 cups of sugar

Pinch of gum arabic

½ cup ground sugar

Sift the flour and put it in a bowl. Cull the semolina and add it to the flour. Add the ground sugar to the gum arabic. It's best to grind them together. Add in all the baking powder and mix well. Then add the 3 cups of oil and whisk all the ingredients together until the oil is absorbed. Add the water, and keep on whisking with one hand until the water is absorbed. Prepare the filling by taking the mashed up dates and making them into 40 small balls. Then thoroughly chop the hazelnuts or almonds. Add in the cinnamon plus the sugar and gum arabic along with the nuts.

With the dough, make ping-pong ball sized chunks and then place them on a plastic tray that has been oiled by hand. Put one teaspoon of the date filling onto each ball. Fashion the dough into concave shapes, with the date filling in the middle. Place into the oven at 375-400 degrees Fahrenheit for 25 minutes. Take out the tray and sprinkle on the sugar-nut topping. Put onto a tray into the refrigerator until it cools down.

Sesame and Anise Cake

عيدي   עידי

INGREDIENTS

2 lbs flour

1 ½ cups corn oil

2 tbsp ground fennel

2 tbsp lightly ground anise

1 tbsp lightly roasted sesame seeds

1 tbsp nigella black seeds

¼ tbsp milk powder

¼ tbsp ground gum arabic

1 tbsp salt

1 oz yeast

2 cups of water

Place all the ingredients except the water into a bowl. Mix so the oil blends well with the rest of the ingredients. After they're all covered in oil, add the water and stir slowly until the dough starts to harden. But don't let it solidify too much. If needed, add an additional quarter-cup of water.

Cover the dough and wait until it expands. Then put it onto a flat surface and flatten it to a quarter-inch thick. Then cut into triangular or square pieces. Put onto a pan and then into the oven preheated to 400 degrees Fahrenheit for 25 minutes. After that, you'll have some really tasty and sweet dessert!

Challah

חלה   فينو

♦ ─────── ♦

INGREDIENTS

(makes 3)

2 lbs flour

4 eggs

4 tbsp sugar

4 oz. raisins

Pinch of salt

¼ cup oil

2 cups water

Roasted sesame seeds

1 tsp rum

1 tsp milk powder

1 tsp gum arabic

2 oz. yeast

Add the flour, salt, sugar, gum arabic, and raisins to a bowl and mix them up. Put the yeast in a half-cup of water and let moisten. In the middle of the bowl, make an indent, where you should place two eggs, oil, and the yeast. Mix this up until the dough becomes smooth and malleable. If needed, add a little bit of water. Cover with a few drops of oil and then cover the bowl.

Let the dough expand for a few hours until it doubles in size. Once this happens, softly knead the dough and let it expand again. After it fully expands, move the dough to the countertop and divide it into 3 equal pieces. From each piece, make 9 rolled strips that are 8-10 inches long and whose ends are thinner than the middles. Now take 3 strips and make a braid out of them like this: Place the three strips side-by-side and braid them together from the middle to the other side. Repeat this with the rest of the sets of strips to make 3 challot.

Place on a baking pan that has been covered by a baking sheet (or in smaller aluminum baking trays for each challah). Wait for the dough to expand one more time. In a small bowl, place the yolk of the 2 remaining eggs, add the rum, and whisk. With a baking brush, spread the egg-rum mix over the dough and sprinkle on the roasted sesame seeds. Bake in an oven at medium heat for 30-40 minutes or until the challot start to brown. Then you'll be ready to serve them up!

ﬡﬧ﬩ﬦﬢ ﬡﬤﬥ ﬡﬦﬦ ﬡﬡ ﬩ﬡﬠﬦ ﬦﬨﬥ ﬤﬥﬡ
ﬡﬠ ﬡ ﬦ ﬤ ﬦﬥ ﬩ ﬡﬨﬡ

[Samaritan script — reproduced as displayed]

ויאמר אלהים הנה נתתי לכם את כל עשב זריע
זרע אשר על פני כל הארץ ואת כל העץ
אשר בו פרי עץ זירע זרע לכם יהיה לאכלה

GOD SAID: "SEE, I GIVE YOU EVERY SEED-BEARING PLANT
THAT IS UPON ALL THE EARTH, AND EVERY
TREE THAT HAS SEED BEARING FRUIT; THEY SHALL BE
YOURS FOR FOOD."

GENESIS 1:29

(SAMARITAN VERSION)

PASSOVER

For thousands of years, the Israelite Samaritans have celebrated the biblical new year, in the spring. On the 14th day of the first month, each year the Samaritans begin the Passover pilgrimage – known in Hebrew as Pesah – by gathering in Kiryat Luza's main square.

The High Priest is accompanied by other distinguished members of the community and important guests from the outside.

Older Samaritans wear prayer attire, while the younger ones don white garments in memory of those who made the biblical exodus from Egypt. The festival is a celebration of rebirth and renewal for the ancient Israelites who escaped bondage.

First, the High Priest – currently Aabed-El ben Aasher from the line of the biblical Kehat in the family of Itamar – recites the sacrificial prayer and announces the ritual slaughter of several dozen sheep (67 in 2020) brought to the altar. Experienced butchers then slaughter the sheep for all to see.

The sheep are prepared before each carcass is put on a spit, with salt rendering them fit. Each spit is then placed into a hot underground oven. Metal grills seal the opening and secure the spits.

With netting, burlap, dirt, and some moist vegetation on top, the flames are stifled and the lamb is roasted until it is well-done.

Recalling the time when the angel of death went to smite the first born sons in Egypt, the Samaritans take the sheep out of the ovens and move them from skewers to large platters. Once the sacrificial lambs are brought to each household, the Samaritans eat the paschal meat quickly with bitter herbs and matzah – unleavened flatbread.

On the seventh day of the festival, the Samaritans observe the Feast of Matzot, the Feast of the Unleavened Bread. On this occasion, members of the community complete the pilgrimage up to Mt. Gerizim, a predawn walk from the synagogue in Kiryat Luza to the summit, while singing and chanting.

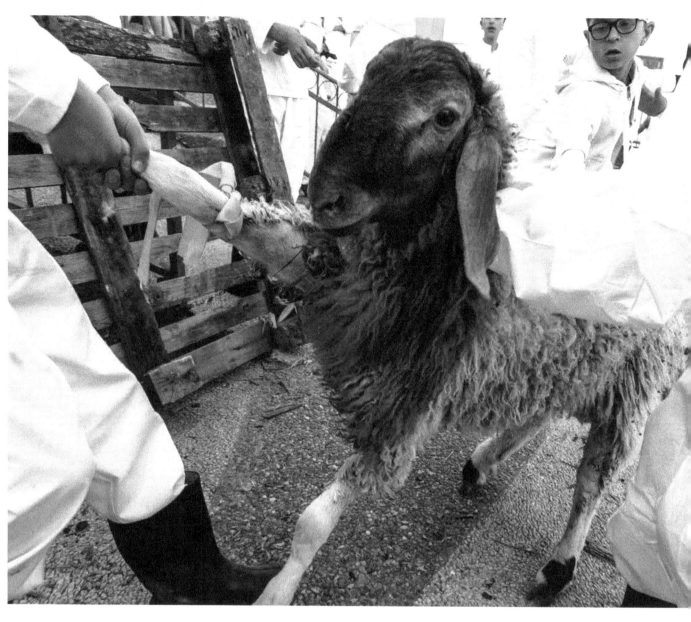

ᏕᎮᎲᏒᎧ ᎧᏝᎧ ᎮᏕᎧᎮᎮ ᎮᎲᎮᏕᎧᏝᎧ ᎧᎮᏕᎮ
ᎧᏝᏕᎮ ᎧᏕ ᎮᎧᎮᎮᏕᎮ ᏕᏕ ᎮᎮᎲᏕᎮᏕᎮ
ᎧᎲᏒᏕᎮᎮ...
ᎮᎲᏒᏒᎮ ᎧᏕᎮ ᎮᏕᏒᏒᎮᏕᎮ ᎧᎲᏕ
ᏕᎮᏒᎧ ᎧᎮᏒᏕᏒ

ואכלו את הבשר בלילה הזה צלי אש ומצות על מררים יאכלהו...
ואכלתם אתו בחפזון פסח הוא לה'

EAT THE MEAT THIS NIGHT ROASTED OVER FIRE; WITH
UNLEAVENED BREAD AND BITTER HERBS… EAT IT HURRIEDLY,
IT IS A PASSOVER OFFERING TO THE LORD.

EXODUS 12: 8, 11

(SAMARITAN VERSION)

HISTORY

Samaritans, as inheritors of Hebrew and Israelite culture, are closely related to Jews. They are the "other Israel," descendants of the Northern tribes of biblical Israel. These include descendants of the tribes of Ephraim, Menashe, and Levi. Samaritans venerate Joseph, the son of Jacob, as their progenitor. With roots in Samaria – rather than Judea, the home of the Jews – they have a unique history and tradition.

The Samaritans have survived huge challenges from biblical times up until the present. The Assyrians conquered the northern Kingdom of Israel in 722 BCE and around one-third of the inhabitants were deported to Mesopotamia. Subsequently, King Sargon II repopulated their part of the Holy Land with people from Babylon in what is now Iraq.

Samaritan scripture consists solely of the Five Books of Moses, the Torah.

Over their 127 generations, countless tragedies struck the Samaritans. Waves of conquerors – including the Byzantine Empire and the Fatimid Caliphate – decimated their numbers. Their community barely survived the early 20th century, but now their numbers are once again increasing. Today the Samaritans number around 850, split almost evenly between Mt. Gerizim and Holon.

15,055. P. Z. – NAPLOUSE. PUITS DE LA SAMARITAINE

Clockwise from top: Prayer before the Passover sacrifice; Samaritan couple; women on Mt. Gerizim, circa 1900

Clockwise from top: Samaritan families; elderly Samaritan; pupils in school

Clockwise from top: Priest leads prayer on Mt. Gerizim;
Samaritan family; high priest inside Nablus synagogue;
Samaritan woman at Jacob's well

Opposite page: young Samaritan girls

POSTSCRIPT

BY PROFESSOR STEVEN FINE

Miriam Altif is an elder of the Israelite Samaritan people. She lives atop Mt. Gerizim, the holy mountain for the Samaritans, above the Palestinian city of Nablus, biblical Shechem.

Her story, told to us in Arabic, was collected by filmmaker Moshe Alafi, of the Yeshiva University Israelite Samaritans Project, to illustrate the story of this remarkable community in their own words and cadence — not just for us, but for the generations of Samaritans to come:

> My father-in-law died when my husband was just a boy of 15 years old, leaving his mother to care for him and five brothers.
>
> They had nothing. He didn't work then, so he begged for money from others, and began to collect donations.
>
> As one of the festivals was coming, his mother said to him: "Your brothers are hungry, they have nothing to eat. Take this tray and go to the shopkeeper. Hock it, and bring me from the proceeds flour to bake bread."
>
> He took the tray and went to the shopkeeper, who refused to give him flour. He cried all the way home.
>
> While walking, the boy came upon something strange, and stepped on it. He thought that it was a mouse.
>
> He looked up to the heavens and said, "Oh, God, I have no money to buy food for my brothers. I certainly have no money to go to the bath house to purify myself. I beg you to have mercy on my brothers, and make sure that I did not step on something that could create still more expenses [by rendering me impure]."

When he went back to see what he had stepped on, the boy saw a pouch on the ground. He picked up the pouch, looked at it in the darkness and saw inside something sparkling.

Taking the pouch, he went on his way. He opened the pouch and found gold coins inside. The boy returned to the shopkeeper and said to him: "Give me flour, rice and sugar."

The shopkeeper asked: "Where did you get this money?" The boy retorted: "God provided it."

My future husband went back to his mother, and his brothers were sleeping. He said to her: "Cook something for them."

She said to him: "But they are sleeping." He then said to her: "Wake them up!" She asked him: "Where did you get this?" He responded: "God gave it."

She cooked for the children, and awakened them, and fed them. The boy paid all the holiday expenses from the contents of the pouch, never counting how much money was inside. At the end of the holiday he found that the sack was empty.

God, O Exalted One, makes sure that no one is left destitute. God gives to those who ask. We thank God for all of His deeds.

Miriam Altif in Kiryat Luza

Miriam's story expresses just how important biblical laws of purity are to the Samaritan community. Touching a dead rodent would have been sufficient to require ritual cleansing at the Turkish bath — an institution of every Islamic city and town.

The sack, its coins sparkling in the darkness of the night and of despair, is a kind of cornucopia, horn of plenty that carries the family through the holiday. The hero of the tale, of course, is God, whom Samaritans call *Shehmaa*, the "Name" in Aramaic — though in her vernacular Arabic Miriam says *Allah*.

The Samaritan religion focuses on the laws of the Torah, the Five Books of Moses. This is their single and all-inspiring holy book. It is written in an ancient Hebrew script that goes back to biblical times. Children memorize the holy text in Samaritan Hebrew by age six.

Samaritans call themselves the "The Keepers," the *Shomrim*, those who preserve and follow the Torah.

Mt. Gerizim is central to Samaritan belief — so much so that the tenth of their Ten Commandments decrees that Samaritans venerate this peak. Their Torah doesn't speak of "the place that the Lord shall choose," as in Jewish (and thus Christian) scripture, but "the place that the Lord has chosen."

Samaritan tradition has it that Noah's ark landed on Mt. Gerizim after the Flood, that the binding of Isaac (Genesis 22) took place on its pinnacle, and that the Tabernacle of *She'ema* once stood on its majestic peak. On holidays the Samaritans assemble in prayer on the holy mountain, and on Passover they make the paschal sacrifice as their ancestors have done for millennia.

The Samaritans possess a rich intellectual tradition, including books of lore and law, exquisite liturgical poetry, Bible study and commentary — written in three languages: Hebrew, Aramaic, and Arabic.

Forced by poverty to sell these precious possessions to curious Westerners, Samaritan manuscripts are today housed in the great libraries of the world.

The dissonance between the life portrayed in Miriam's tale and the lives of contemporary Samaritans is profound and even bewildering. The twentieth century witnessed a renaissance of Samaritan life that continues to our day.

British and American Protestants did much in support of the community during the nineteenth century. Zionism and the State of Israel have provided rich soil and real resources for the resurgence of this small "branch of Ephraim" (Ezekiel 37:16). The community has blossomed.

This cookbook documents the rich culture of the Samaritans in a most delicious way — viewed outward from the kitchens and dining rooms of its families. We see here a medley of Near Eastern recipes, and more importantly, the people who enjoy them.

We are invited into their homes, their synagogues, history, and celebrations. A true joy — and thankfully, there's no more hunger!

Told today, Miriam's story reminds young Samaritans of the faith of their ancestors, and how through that faith they prevailed over their own extinction. Her tale is a letter from the older generation of "the Keepers," to their children and grandchildren. It is also a message of hope for us. As she puts it, "God gives to those who ask."

Steven Fine is the Dean Pinkhos Churgin Professor of Jewish History at Yeshiva University, director of the YU Center for Israel Studies and the YU Israelite Samaritans Project.

For Further Reading:
Steven Fine, ed., *The Samaritans: A Biblical People*, Boston: Brill and New York: Yeshiva University Press, 2021.
Reinhard Pummer, *The Samaritans: A Profile*, Grand Rapids MI: Eerdmans, 2016.

ואכלת ושבעת וברכת את ה' אלהיך על הארץ הטבה
אשר נתן לך

WHEN YOU HAVE EATEN YOUR FILL, BLESS THE LORD YOUR
GOD FOR THE GOOD LAND THAT HE HAS GIVEN YOU.

DEUTERONOMY 8:10

(SAMARITAN VERSION)

IMAGE SOURCES

All photos by Yadid Levi unless otherwise noted:

Citations are shown in the order that the photographs appear in the book

Gezer Calendar. Yoav Dothan, 2012. Wikimedia Commons

Shekel of Israel. Judaea, First Jewish War. Dated year 3 (68/69 CE) Classical Numismatic Group

Samaritan mezuzah, Mount Gerizim. Avi Deror, 2013. Wikimedia Commons

The well of the Samaritan, ca. 1900. Library of Congress

Prayer before the sacrifice, ca. 1900-1910. National Library of Israel, Photo Collection

Samaritan man and wife, ca. 1900-1910. National Library of Israel, Photo Collection

Samaritan women on summit of Mt. Gerizim during prayer, ca. 1900-1910. National Library of Israel, Photo
Collection

Samaritan bachelors and girls they are waiting for to grow up, ca. 1900-1910. National Library of Israel,
Photo Collection

Old Samaritan, ca. 1900-1920. Dry plate negative. Library of Congress

Samaritan school, ca. 1900-1920. Dry plate negative. Nablus. Library of Congress

Samaritan high priest raises a Torah scroll, ca. 1900-1910. National Library of Israel, Photo Collection

The Samaritans, B.W. Kilburn, ca. 1899. Library of Congress

Interior of the synagogue of the Samaritans, Nablus, ca. 1920. Wikimedia Commons

A Samaritan woman at Jacob's well, Palestine, Underwood & Underwood, ca. 1900. Lenkin Family
Collection of Photography, Penn Libraries

Samaritan young maidens, ca. 1900-1910. National Library of Israel, Photo Collection

Samaritan prayer on Mt. Gerizim, ca. 1900-1910. National Library of Israel, Photo Collection

---

Yeshiva University
CENTER FOR ISRAEL STUDIES

The Samaritan Cookbook is a proud partner
of the Yeshiva University Israelite Samaritans Project.

We are grateful to Wipf and Stock Publishers and also would like to thank our wives – Miriam, Z-Z, and Dana – for always encouraging us along the way. Many thanks as well to our One Semitistan board for their insights and support on the Samaritan Cookbook project.

SAMARITAN COOKBOOK

A Culinary Odyssey from the Ancient Israelites to the Modern Mediterranean

Copyright © 2020 Benyamim Tsedaka, Ben Piven, and Avishay Zelmanovich

Wipf & Stock
An Imprint of Wipf and Stock Publishers
199 W. 8th Ave., Suite 3
Eugene, OR 97401

www.wipfandstock.com

PAPERBACK ISBN: 978-1-7252-8589-7
HARDCOVER ISBN: 978-1-7252-8588-0
EBOOK ISBN: 978-1-7252-8590-3

ABOUT THE CREATORS

Benyamim Tsedaka is an elder of his people and head of the Israelite Samaritan Information Center. He has published more than 120 books and over 2,000 articles on Samaritan life.

He was born in 1944 in Nablus, and since 1966, he has hosted tourists and educational groups visiting Samaritan sites in Holon and Mt. Gerizim. He completed studies in the History of the People of Israel, and Bible Studies, at the Hebrew University of Jerusalem. Since 1969, he has been chief editor of newspaper A.B The Samaritan News.

Beginning in 1980, he served as choir director for the Israelite Samaritan Music Ensemble and chairman of the Samaritan basketball team.

He runs the A.B Institute of Samaritan Studies and teaches globally about Samaritans in Hebrew, Arabic, and English. In 1985, he founded the Society of Samaritan Studies. He runs the Samaritan Medal Committee for Peace and Humanitarian Achievements. Tsedaka has published the Israelite Samaritan version of the Torah with side-by-side translations of the Samaritan and Jewish Pentateuch.

Ben Piven has spent over a decade as a journalist for Al Jazeera and other outlets. With extensive experience in the languages and societies of the Middle East, the Baltimore native was a Fulbright Scholar in cultural geography. He studied digital media at Columbia University School of Journalism.

Avishay Zelmanovich is a scholar of Middle Eastern cultures and Jewish history. Being fluent in Hebrew and English helped him translate the complexities of the original cookbook. Born in Kibbutz Na'an but raised in New York, he has bridged the American and Israeli cultural landscapes.

In 2007, the Samaritan Cookbook editors met Benyamim "Benny" Tsedaka at his home in Holon and then attended the Passover celebration for the Samaritan community in Kiryat Luza atop Mt. Gerizim.

For Ben, interest in Samaritan history turned from an initial newspaper assignment to a long-term passion when he and Avishay began to rendezvous with Benny during the Samaritan lecturer's annual U.S. trips.

The author, Benyamim Tsedaka, and editors, Avishay Zelmanovich and Ben Piven, discuss the Samaritan Cookbook in New York City in 2015.

For more information, visit our website SamaritanCookbook.com Find Samaritan Cookbook on Facebook, Instagram, Twitter, and YouTube.

Printed in the USA
CPSIA information can be obtained
at www.ICGtesting.com
LVHW070217141023
760774LV00090B/120